Merry Christmas 12/25/18
And
Happy New Year 2019

Love,

Copy: Corinne Burgermeister, Kate Dale, Michael Fiez, Rob Gard, Ellen Larson, Anna Shircel, Amber Wiza
Images: Focal Flame Photography
Book and Cover Design: Amy LaPlante, Nicky Brillowski/KCI Sports Publishing
Publisher: Peter J. Clark/KCI Sports Publishing
Additional Images: Bryce Richter/University of Wisconsin-Madison (page 17),
Social media submissions (pages 66-67, 118-125)
Tammy King (page 70), University of Wisconsin-Madison (page 9)

Visit the Bucky on Parade website at buckyonparade.com.

ISBN: 978-1-940056-61-6

Printed in the United States of America
KCI Sports Publishing   3340 Whiting Avenue, Suite 5   Stevens Point, WI 54481
Phone: 1-800-697-3756   Fax: 715-344-2668
www.kcisports.com

Bucky on Parade. I first heard that phrase in 2004. Back then, it was a broad stroke. An abstract idea. How could we, as an organization that represents the Greater Madison area, show how much we love our community, and show how much our community, our state, loves Bucky Badger?

In 2017, we finally saw our opportunity. Local leaders came together with a shared vision of what we wanted to accomplish: one of the largest public art events in the country, celebrating the spirit and the many different personas of Bucky and our community.

Over the next 16 months, the logistics of this project came together thanks to an unprecedented partnership between the Madison Area Sports Commission, the Greater Madison Convention & Visitors Bureau, the University of Wisconsin Chancellor's office, UW Athletics, Wisconsin Foundation & Alumni Association, city officials, county officials, local businesses and Madison College. And those logistics were managed by staff and committee members who worked tirelessly to bring the blueprint to reality.

Two goals emerged from our planning process. The first was that this project needed to be open to artistic interpretation with minimal guidelines. As Bucky means so many different things to so many different people, we wanted to encourage and celebrate the diversity of unique interpretations. The second goal, and most important, was that the parade needed to be bigger than Bucky, bigger than Madison and go beyond the public art perspective and provide a meaningful legacy.

Garding Against Cancer met that goal. Knowing that proceeds raised from the parade were going to help people throughout Wisconsin who were dealing with cancer, as well as help their families and caretakers, inspired sponsors, artists, staff and everyone involved throughout the process. Selecting the Garding Against Cancer initiative as the charity of choice was easy.

Bucky on Parade opened to the public on May 7, 2018, as all the statues were unveiled simultaneously throughout Dane County. Any hope we had of the parade's success was dwarfed by the immediate response. Tens of thousands of photos shared on social media. Visitors from around the country awed by the incredibly detailed statues. Parents thanking us on a daily basis for giving their kids something really cool to do all summer. And hearing the voices of those kids, every single day, shout with joy as they spotted a new Bucky, and loudly proclaiming their favorite as they walked around the Capitol Square.

The following pages provide a brief glimpse of what Bucky on Parade was during the summer of 2018. It's a colorful reminder that no matter who we are, where we're from, what we do or what we believe, there are things in this world that will still unite us and create a shared bond. Thank you, Bucky!

— Deb Archer, President and CEO, Madison Area Sports Commission
and Greater Madison Convention & Visitors Bureau

TAKING BUCKY TO THE STREETS OF MADISON

I confess: I love Bucky Badger. Not only is he a great mascot who cheers our teams on the field, he also shows up for student award ceremonies, he is here to welcome new students to campus and to help make important public service announcements.

One of my favorite evenings is Halloween, when Bucky comes to my house and passes out candy to all the trick-or-treaters. The way children respond to Bucky is wonderful to watch.

In short, Bucky Badger is much more than a mascot to us; he's a symbol of one of the greatest universities in the world. Sometimes you see the competitive Bucky, sometimes the serious Bucky and sometimes the goofy Bucky. But in any season, and in any form, Bucky Badger is Wisconsin through and through.

So it is fitting that this summer Madison was overrun with Buckys — 85 of them to be exact — each decorated with a different theme. Bucky Badger is immediately recognizable by everyone — whether they attended UW–Madison or not.

The wonderful thing about public art is that it's out there for the entire community to enjoy. That's why the Bucky on Parade art project was so successful. I've loved watching people of all ages inspect the design on a Bucky statue and then snap a picture with him.

I'm delighted to have UW-Madison represented in 85 different ways around town. I hope you've enjoyed the exhibit as much as I have.

— Rebecca Blank, UW-Madison Chancellor

THE EVOLUTION OF
Bucky Badger

Wisconsin's loveable mascot, Bucky Badger, has always ranked high in fan appeal and enthusiasm. Although badgers in various forms had been the University of Wisconsin mascot for decades, the version that is currently known as Bucky, sporting a cardinal and white sweater, was first drawn in 1940. In 1949, a student first wore a badger outfit with a papier-máchê head at the homecoming game and the mascot came to life.

The nickname "Badgers," was borrowed from the state of Wisconsin, which was dubbed the "Badger State." The name didn't come from the animals in the region, but rather from an association with lead miners in the 1820s. Without shelter in the winter, the miners had to "live like Badgers" in tunnels burrowed into hillsides.

The badger started as the official UW mascot with the inception of intercollegiate football in 1889. The original live badger mascot was too vicious to control. On more than one occasion, the live badger escaped handlers before a sideline hero recaptured the animal with a flying tackle. It was decided in the interest of fan and player safety that Wisconsin's mascot be retired to the Madison Zoo.

In 1949, a student in the university's art department was commissioned to mold a papier-máchê badger head, and the beloved badger made his first full-costumed appearance. At that time, the badger went by names like Benny, Buddy, Bernie, Bobby and Bouncey. A contest was staged to name the popular mascot. The winner was Buckingham U. Badger, or Bucky. The name apparently came from the lyrics in a song which encouraged the football team to "buck right through that line."

There are approximately seven students needed to meet the more than 700 Bucky Badger appearances each year. From sporting events to community service requests to the occasional wedding, Bucky is a popular and enduring fixture among Wisconsin fans.

— Courtesy of the UW Athletic Department

WHAT IS BUCKY ON PARADE?

Bucky on Parade is a community collaboration that has been in the works for many years. Inspired by CowParade Wisconsin (2006) and Iowa City's Herky on Parade (2004 and 2014), this public art event was born out of the overwhelming love for Wisconsin's favorite mascot, Bucky Badger. The project brought 85 life-sized Bucky statues, transformed into beautiful and fun pieces of art, to the streets of Madison and Dane County from May 7 to September 12, 2018. In addition to being a community event for all to enjoy, Bucky on Parade raised funds to support two primary organizations — Garding Against Cancer and the Madison Area Sports Commission, in addition to various other community charities.

Bucky Badger is a Wisconsin icon and was proudly created by a Wisconsin manufacturer. The statues were designed and produced by FAST Corporation in Sparta, WI. Each six-foot-tall statue was crafted from fiberglass and weighs 118 pounds. The blank fiberglass statues arrived in Madison in January 2018 and were distributed to local and regional artists to begin the design process.

TRANSFORMING INTO WORKS OF ART

Over 200 statue designs were submitted for consideration as part of Bucky on Parade. Of the hundreds of submissions, 64 artists were chosen to make 85 unique designs come to life. The selected group of professional and amateur artists ranged from teachers and students to an anesthesiologist, a medical director, a political cartoonist and a tattoo artist.

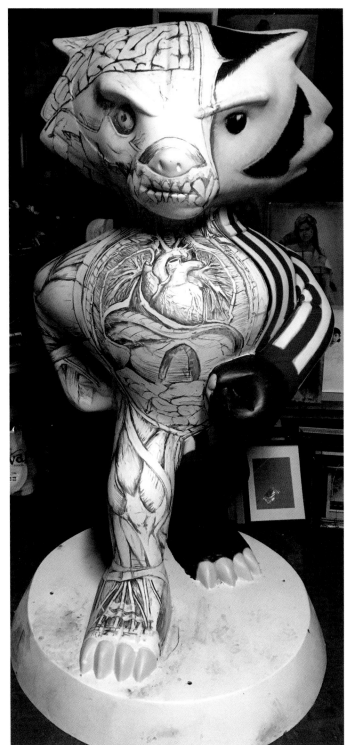

IT'S TIME TO PARADE!

On the evening of May 6, the statues were installed throughout Dane County, including Madison, Monona, Middleton, Sun Prairie, Fitchburg and Verona. The installation process was a team effort with major contributions from Lycon, TWO MEN AND A TRUCK, JP Cullen and Madison College. The statues were wrapped in black plastic to conceal the design until the official unveil the following morning.

UNVEILING THE STATUES

With the help of artists, sponsors and hundreds of supporters, Bucky on Parade statues were unveiled simultaneously to the public on May 7. Following the unveiling, Bucky Badger and the UW Marching Band led a community celebration at the top of State Street to reveal the final two statues. Crazylegs Bucky was unveiled at a later date, which brought together many fans to celebrate the love for Bucky on Parade.

Meet THE STATUES

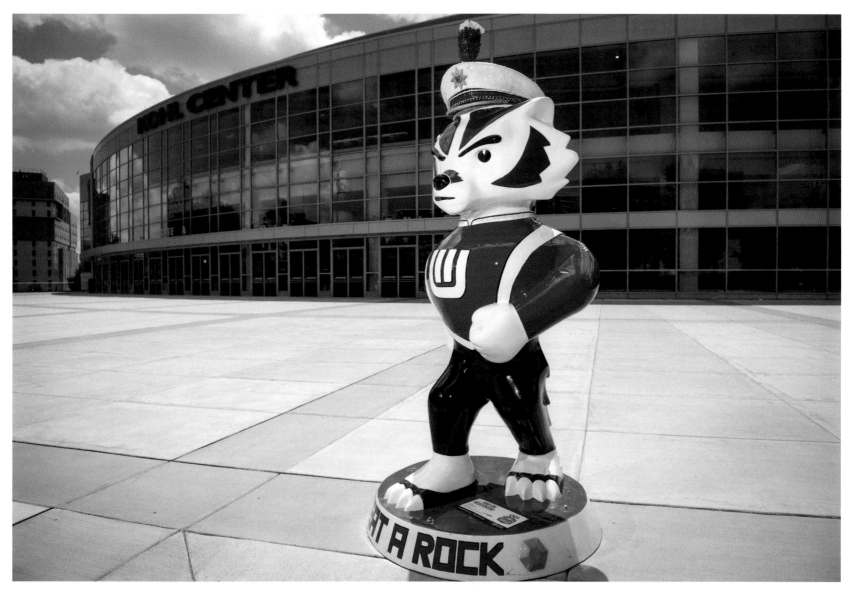

As UW Band Director Michael Leckrone says, "When you're in the band, you've got to be tough enough to eat a rock!" This statue represents past, present and future members of the UW Marching Band. The artist, a Stevens Point native, only took one drawing class while studying at UW-Madison, but has continued to fuel her interest in art by taking on projects for friends and family.

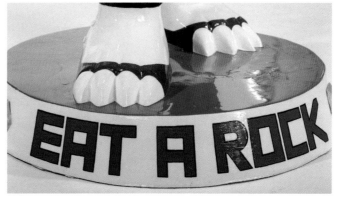

#GAMEDAYBUCKY

Artists: Rose Malm with Austin Fath
Sponsor: University Book Store

It's not Game Day without a pair of bibs! Bucky is ready to cheer on the team with his red and white overalls, Jump Around shirt and Motion "W" tattoo.

Bucky is dressed in his shoulder pads and football jersey, ready to step on the field at Camp Randall Stadium. As the team advances down the field, the crowd responds, "1st and 10, Wisconsin!"

5TH QUARTER

Artist: Kim Marie
Sponsor: Lands' End

Join the UW Marching Band for everyone's favorite quarter in college football! This statue is decoupaged with actual sheet music, and real band instruments are attached to the base.

Artist: James McKiernan
Sponsor: Madison Festivals, Inc.

A TASTE OF MADISON

This statue provides a "taste" of Madison, as it depicts some of the city's most-visited locations, including the lakes, the city skyline and our favorite sporting events.

DID YOU KNOW?

Held since 1983, the Taste of Madison event features over 80 restaurants, three entertainment stages and draws over 250,000 people to the Capitol Square every Labor Day weekend.

ALL HANDS ON BUCKY

Artist: Ann Pahnke
Sponsor: CUNA Mutual Group

The children who provided the hand prints covering this statue are from the Milwaukee Sign Language School. This project brought them closer to the city of Madison and UW-Madison through Bucky. The artist said the mascot represents joy, optimism and inclusion in education.

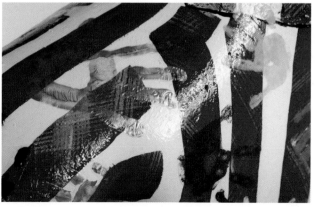

DID YOU KNOW?

The youngest known student to graduate from UW-Madison was then 16-year-old Serra Crawford in 2012.

Two well-known symbols come together for the ultimate ode to Wisconsin. The artwork on Bucky shows a life-like Holstein cow, representing the state's thriving dairy industry.

ANIMALS NEED BUCKY TOO

Artist: Kathy King
Sponsors: The BerbeeWalsh Foundation and Debbie Cervenka

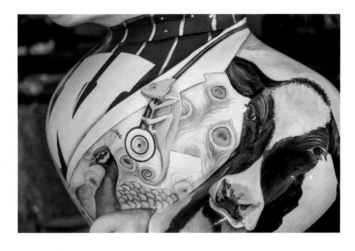

Everything from family pets to zoo animals form a collage on this Bucky. The statue deserves a close look to find all of the creatures big and small surrounding his arms and legs. Fun fact: Many of the animals represent real pets!

Bucky is suited up, with a basketball under his arm, and is ready to take to the court! This statue's base is made to look like a basketball and he guarded UW-Madison's iconic Red Gym during the Parade.

BETWEEN THE LAKES

Artist: Amy Mietzel
Sponsors: The QTI Group & Stone House Development

Between the Lakes celebrates Madison's unique status as one of only two major cities in the United States to be situated on an isthmus. The Capitol on this colorful Bucky sits proudly against a radiant Wisconsin sun, as the blue waters ripple up Bucky's legs.

Artist: Karen Hitchcock
Sponsor: Fitchburg Chamber Visitor + Business Bureau

BIKE THE 'BURG BUCKY

Meet avid biker Bucky. One of his favorite places to ride? Fitchburg! He's covered with landmarks and the beautiful scenery bikers encounter while pedaling around the 'Burg.

DID YOU KNOW?

The Badger State Trail is a 40-mile trail extending from Fitchburg to the Illinois state line. This ride takes you through beautiful Wisconsin communities with scenery of bluffs, old train depots and miles of wildflowers.

BIOTECH BUCKY

Artist: Christy Grace
Sponsor: Fitchburg Community & Economic Development Authority

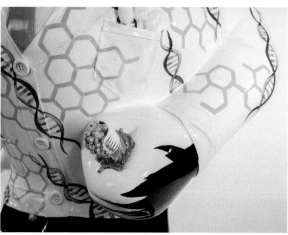

With his goggles and white coat, Bucky is ready to spend the day in the lab. This statue speaks to the curiosity in all of us — especially students, teachers and the next generation of scientists!

Artist: Phil Hands
Sponsor: Wisconsin State Journal/madison.com

BLACK, WHITE AND "READ" ALL OVER

Dressed in his classic striped sweater, this statue is adorned with cheerful cartoons of Bucky partaking in some of Madison's popular pastimes, including college sports, biking, Ultimate Frisbee and winter activities. As a political cartoonist, the artist is used to creating work about contentious political issues. Drawing Bucky gave him the opportunity to create something everyone can enjoy.

BLOOMING BUCKY

Artists: Paula Hare & Diane Heatley

Bucky is in full bloom! This statue is inspired by native Wisconsin prairies and wildflowers, and is covered in lush green foliage and beautiful blossoms.

This Northwoods-themed Bucky was created in mosaic, using a variety of stained glass tiles. The axe in his left hand is symbolic of the famous border battle between the Wisconsin Badgers and Minnesota Gophers football teams, dating back to 1890.

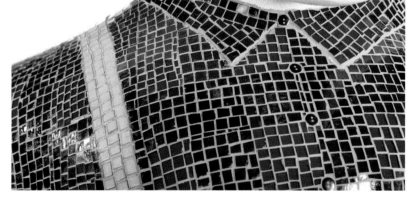

BRIGHT IDEA BUCKY

Artist: Kathryn Schnabel
Sponsor: Capitol Lakes

Bright Idea Bucky captures the spirit of excitement and optimism about what the future can hold. This statue was completed in an art studio, with visitors' written ideas and inspirations incorporated onto the fabric.

34

Bucky Badger here, coming to you live from Madison. Broadcaster Bucky keeps the community informed about the news, sports and events they love.

DID YOU KNOW?

Several well-known journalists are UW-Madison alumni, including Peter Greenberg, Andy Katz, Jeff Greenfield, Lynsey Addario and Rita Braver.

Artist: Dan Gardiner
Sponsor: Hottmann Construction Company, Inc.

BUCK-Y BADGER

This buck-themed Bucky pays homage to a popular Wisconsin tradition: deer hunting. But don't worry, this 6-foot Buck-y will be safe in his red-and-white striped sweater.

BUCKY ALVAREZ

Artist: Dan Gardiner
Sponsor: UW Athletics

This statue will make you do a double take! Bucky dons a pair of khakis, red sweater vest and a headset to mirror his namesake, and is ready to coach the team.

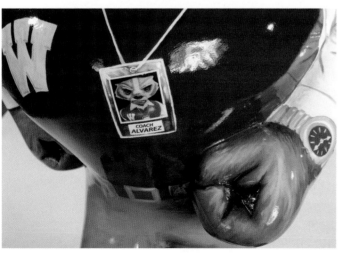

This statue captures all aspects of the Memorial Union Terrace, from the iconic Sunburst chair, to the lake with a sailboat and a sunny sky with dashes of color from the setting sun.

BUCKY BOT

Artist: Jeff Dewitt
Sponsor: Madison College

Bucky Bot is ready for the future with his intricate, mechanical suit and superhuman abilities. With books in hand and wearing a Madison College shirt, he's ready to take on the world. The artist behind Bucky Bot is the co-director of the animation and concept development department at Madison College.

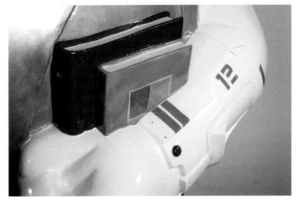

As its name suggests, this statue is inspired by Picasso. The design incorporates cubism, lots of bright colors and whimsy and fittingly, lived in front of the Chazen Museum of Art during the Parade.

BUCKY DE LOS MUERTOS

Artist: Jennifer Estelle Schwarzkopf

This statue celebrates the vibrant colors, richness and celebration of life that is El Día de los Muertos. The design reflects the culture of Madisonians of Latino heritage, while providing an opportunity for those unfamiliar with the celebration to learn about a different tradition. Bucky de los Muertos reminds us of the importance of remembrance, family and community.

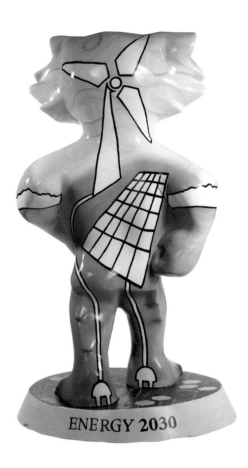

Inspired by the sponsor, this statue features an electric car, solar panel sunglasses and lots of sunshine. It incorporates the passions and dreams for the good of the future Madison.

BUCKY HOW'D YOU GET SO FLY?

Artist: Emily Liefke
Sponsor: WHEELS UP

Bucky, Bucky how'd you get so fly? With his aviator sunglasses and pilot wings, Captain Bucky is prepared for take off and ready to fly to a far-off destination.

Artist: FAST Corporation
Sponsor: Three Bears Resort

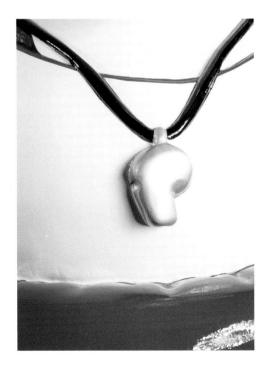

There's nothing like summer in Wisconsin. With his whistle, swim trunks and inner tube, Bucky is all set for a day at the pool.

BUCKY IN RED

Artist: Savannah Guthrie

The artwork on this statue is inspired by Russian folk art and was intricately hand-painted to resemble a beautiful piece of pottery. The traditional color is blue, but for Bucky it had to be red!

Artist: Rob Severson
Sponsor: Oak Park Place

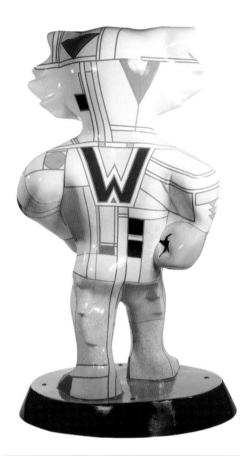

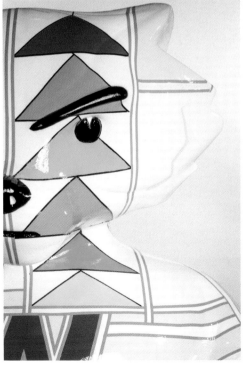

This tribute to Wisconsin native Frank Lloyd Wright includes a classic W, which compliments the aesthetics associated with the stained glass work of the renowned architect. During the Parade, this Bucky resided on the rooftop of the Wright-designed Monona Terrace.

BUCKY ON GUARD

Artist: Christy Rasmussen
Sponsor: TWO MEN AND A TRUCK

Bucky on Guard is guarding all the traditions, treasures and landmarks of Madison. This artwork came to life in a middle school art studio in Merrill, WI, where students were able to watch their teacher's progress and be involved in the excitement and community aspect of Bucky on Parade, even from over 100 miles away.

"BUCKY'S HOME MAY BE ON THE UW-MADISON CAMPUS, BUT *the* *reach* OF BUCKY ON PARADE HAS BEEN FELT THROUGHOUT DANE COUNTY, THE STATE OF WISCONSIN AND BEYOND."

- REBECCA BLANK, UW-MADISON CHANCELLOR

Artist: Dan Gardiner
Sponsor: WMTV – NBC15

Head down John Nolen Drive in the colder months and you will see the frozen lake dotted with ice fishermen waiting for a bite. Bucky on Ice celebrates one of Madison's most popular winter sports.

Artist: Erica Vetrovec
Sponsor: Dave Jones, Inc.

With wrench in hand and tool belt securely fastened, Bucky is ready to tackle any and all plumbing repairs — starting with the leaky pipes under his feet!

DID YOU KNOW?

The Red Gym on the UW-Madison campus was built in 1894 as a militia training and student recreation center. It's now on the National Register of Historic Places.

The traditional Bucky we all know and love was hand-painted to create a triangulated, multi-dimensional appearance. The artwork was a collaborative effort by employees at Filament Games, a company that makes video games by trade and continues the creativity after-hours. Everyone from formally-trained digital artists to untrained producers helped create this statue.

Bucky is out of this world! This statue is covered with swirling celestial bodies, accented with glittery, glow-in-the-dark paint and a "W" made of stars.

CLASS ACT

Artist: Barbara Vater
Sponsor: Park Hotel

Bucky sure does clean up nicely! This statue features him with his best outfit on, and he's all ready for his big debut.

Artist: Richard Yanke
Sponsor: Oakland on Monroe and Gregg Shimanski Realty, Inc.

Elroy Leon "Crazylegs" Hirsch played at UW-Madison as a halfback and then served as the athletic director from 1969 to 1987. He earned the nickname "Crazylegs" for his unusual running style and this Bucky honors Hirsch with a unique mold.

DREAM BIG BUCKY

Artist: Jaroslava Sobiskova

Dream Big Bucky is inspired by the hopes and dreams of the children at American Family Children's Hospital. Many of the drawings were sketched by children, which the artist brought to life on the statue, adding color and additional images to complete the design. This statue is warm, comforting and reminds us all to dream big.

ENLIGHTENED BUCKY

Artist: Lon Michels
Sponsor: Culver's Foundation

This statue is covered from head to toe with brightly-colored, intricate butterflies which often represent enlightenment in literature and academia. Without Bucky the academic, we wouldn't have Bucky the mascot.

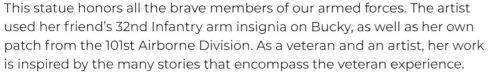

This statue honors all the brave members of our armed forces. The artist used her friend's 32nd Infantry arm insignia on Bucky, as well as her own patch from the 101st Airborne Division. As a veteran and an artist, her work is inspired by the many stories that encompass the veteran experience.

FARMER BUCKY

Artist: Julie Hancock
Sponsor: Lycon

Can you guess how many farms cover Wisconsin? More than 68,000! Farmer Bucky pays homage to the hardworking farmers who produce the delicious food we love to eat.

FLAMINGO BUCKY

This statue is covered in painterly flamingos in a field of flowers, inspired by the beloved UW-Madison tradition of filling Bascom Hill with flamingos each year!

DID YOU KNOW?

Every year, hundreds of pink plastic flamingos roost on UW-Madison's Bascom Hill. Although this tradition has become a fundraiser for the university, it began decades ago as a prank. Pail & Shovel was a student political organization that stirred up campus with pranks in the 1970s and 1980s, most famously planting 1,008 flamingos on Bascom Hill and building a statue of a drowning Statue of Liberty on Lake Mendota, both in 1979.

FRIDAY NIGHT FISH FRY

Artist: Ashley Sheridan
Sponsor: The Edgewater

Bucky has returned from catching his dinner, just in time to enjoy a traditional Wisconsin Friday Night Fish Fry. Bucky has all he needs, with a fishing pole in his hand, a vintage basket over his shoulder and his Friday Fish Fry menu at his feet. Bucky stands on a traditional relish tray base, complete with carrots, olives, radishes, peppers and pickles.

Bucky's uniform is a collage of every branch of the service since the Vietnam War. Material from actual uniforms was used and adhered with glue and sewing connections. The face and other non-clothed portions are covered with scenes and sayings significant to the veterans who completed the artwork. The base is covered with acrylic paint and textured sand, and the boots use real laces. A representation of the U.S. flag is tucked under Bucky's arm. The group of artists that created this statue is made up of military veterans from all branches and various generations. The group was formed as a partnership between Very Special Arts Wisconsin and the Madison Vet Center. The veterans involved see art not only as a hobby, but as a version of therapy and way of coping with their life stressors and military traumas.

FUNKY BUCKINGHAM

Artist: Kim Marie
Sponsor: Greenway Station Shopping Center

Household items (like potato mashers and bubble wrap) were used to apply acrylic paint in a random, funky pattern over the entire statue. Hand-painted details are incorporated into the Motion "W" design on the front and the Badger paw design on the back.

Dressed in his Badger lederhosen, this Bucky embodies Gemütlichkeit — a feeling of friendship, warmth and good cheer.

GOLDEN BUCKY

Golden Bucky was the only statue to move locations during the Parade, making a picture with him extra special! His appearances ranged from schools, pools and the Henry Vilas Zoo to some of greater Madison's largest events.

GOODNIGHT BUCKY

Artist: Angelica Contreras

This statue was inspired by Wisconsinites' love of camping and nature, and was fittingly located at UW-Madison's Picnic Point entrance during the Parade. The design features images of people and woodland creatures enjoying the great, peaceful outdoors under a starry sky.

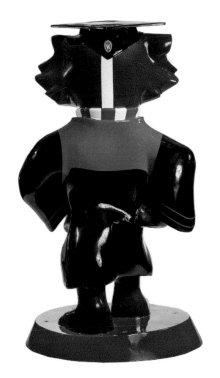

Dressed in cap and gown, with a diploma in hand, this Bucky is ready to celebrate his graduation. He spent the Parade perched on top of UW-Madison's Bascom Hill and was designed by FAST Corporation, the company that manufactured all of the Bucky on Parade statues.

Bucky is decked out in red and ready to shoot some hoops! This statue is named after the enthusiastic student section who cheer for the Badgers from behind the basket at the Kohl Center.

GROW

Artist: Emmalee Pearson
Sponsor: Madison College

Grow showcases the entire flower, from its luscious, red bloom to its roots crawling down Bucky's legs. Textured and life-like, the roots cover the base and connect the flowers to the cloud-covered sky.

Peace, love and Bucky! This groovy statue embodies all things '70s, with peace signs, tie dye, smiley-faces and even a soul patch and ponytail combination. Do you spot the iconic Madison pink flamingo hiding behind his leg?

I AM BUCKY

Artist: Insane Paint Shop

We can all see ourselves in Bucky – literally. This statue is spray-painted a shiny, chrome color, providing a mirror-like finish. Insane Paint Shop is an automotive customization shop and used Cosmichrome, a spray-on chrome paint, to create this stunning piece.

This statue imagines what's underneath the classic red-and-white striped sweater, depicting Bucky with a variety of Madison-themed tattoos. The artist's previous community art projects include a fiberglass cow and giraffe.

IT TAKES TWO WHEELS

Artist: Brooke Wentland

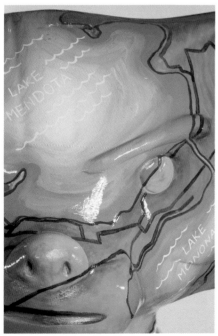

It Takes Two Wheels draws inspiration from Madison's vibrant biking community. Several bike trails are depicted, along with some key trail features, including one of the tunnels near Belleville, WI. The base of the statue is painted to resemble a bicycle wheel.

It's said in Madison there are two seasons: winter and construction. This statue celebrates the beauty that comes from beyond the orange barrel. This hard-working Bucky features construction scenes, iconic Madison spots and the beauty of Wisconsin's seasons.

JUMP AROUND BUCKY

Artist: Karen Lorraine Singer
Sponsor: The Great Dane Pub & Brewing Company

This statue pays homage to one of the greatest traditions in college football: Jump Around! It's covered with photos of fans at Camp Randall, including the student section.

"THE PUBLIC RESPONSE TO BUCKY ON PARADE WAS BEYOND OUR WILDEST EXPECTATIONS AND WENT BEYOND THE ENCHANTMENT OF THE FABULOUS STATUES. RESIDENTS AND VISITORS EXPLORED NEIGHBORHOODS THAT THEY MIGHT NOT OTHERWISE SEE, SHOPPED AT BUSINESSES THEY NEVER KNEW ABOUT AND *shared an experience* THEY'LL CHERISH FOR YEARS TO COME."

- DEB ARCHER, PRESIDENT AND CEO OF THE
MADISON AREA SPORTS COMMISSION AND
GREATER MADISON CONVENTION & VISITORS BUREAU

LECKRONE'S STOP AT THE TOP

Artist: Jeanne Burgess
Sponsor: JP Cullen

This design was inspired by UW band director Michael Leckrone and all of the fun he has brought to UW-Madison. Many may not know that Leckrone created the bands signature step, "stop at the top," and this statue was uniquely molded with a raised knee.

Artist: Emily J. Wirkus
Sponsor: Underwood Events

LUCKY BUCKY

Lucky Bucky is made of 11,759 Lincoln pennies, all facing heads up — with a few exceptions. One of each type of penny is showing the tail side: Wheat, Lincoln Memorial, Lincoln Bicentennial, 2009 (four designs) and Union Shield. There's even a no-longer-minted Canadian penny in the mix.

Artist: Aislen Kelly
Sponsors: Downtown Madison Inc. and
Madison's Central Business Improvement District

Welcome to fabulous Madison, Wisconsin! This statue honors some of Madison's most loved locations like the State Capitol and Memorial Union Terrace. The base features a variety of Wisconsin's favorite food — cheese!

The drum major is the leader of the marching band, and Major Bucky leads the way with striking artwork and fiberglass additions for his outfit and baton. His hat makes him especially tall and he was easy to spot overlooking the UW Marching Band practice fields during the Parade.

Artist: Jaroslava Sobiskova
Sponsor: The William, Deborah, Kelly and Colleen Flesch Family

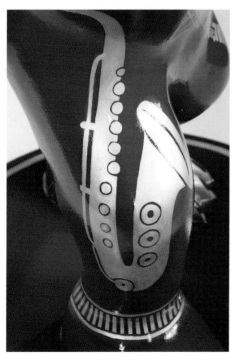

A saxophone, trumpet, tuba, trombone and more are featured on this instrument-themed statue that's painted Badger red.

ONE LEG UP

Fill the hill! The pink flamingos are out in full force, atop a green base representing Bascom Hill located in the heart of the UW-Madison campus. Fun fact: the turf on the base came directly from Camp Randall Stadium.

OUR HEARTS BELONG TO BUCKY

Artist: Roxanne Robinson

The abundance of red hearts on Our Hearts Belong to Bucky symbolize the love so many feel toward Bucky Badger. It also gives the impression of stained glass, which affects how we see the light that comes in.

Artist: Anne Raskopf
Sponsor: The Madison Concourse Hotel and Governor's Club

This statue features everything we love about Wisconsin, all on one Bucky! From the farmers' markets, to fishing, to Sunday drives — there's something for everyone.

PUCKY

Artist: Dan Gardiner
Sponsor: J.H. Findorff & Son Inc.

Drop the puck! Bucky's skates are laced up, and he's ready for the big game. With a real hockey stick in hand and hockey puck on the base, this athletic badger celebrates one of Wisconsin's favorite sports.

DID YOU KNOW?

The UW-Madison men's hockey program has won six national championships, and the UW women's program has captured four national championships since 2006.

Artist: Matt Smith
Sponsor: John and Jeanne Flesch

Bucky is covered in silver sequined fabric that was cut, tightly fitted piece by piece and fully glued to the form. With the contours and reflectivity of the fabric, the statue grabs and reflects light and passing colors. There is also one red sequin hidden among the silver!

Artist: S. V. Medaris
Sponsor: Wisconsin Foundation and Alumni Association

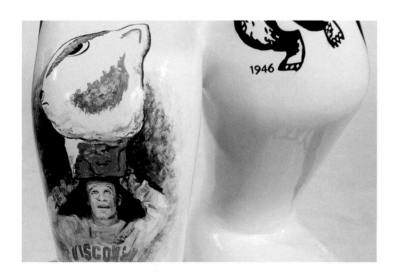

Inspired by a love of everything Bucky, this statue dons the traditional red and white sweater, and features various iterations of the beloved mascot through the years.

"(SLAPS HANDS AGAINST HIS HEAD.) (RAISES HIS ARMS TO THE SKY). (CLINGS HIS HANDS TO HIS HEART). (HIGH FIVES THE PERSON WHO ASKED HIM HOW HE FEELS ABOUT BUCKY ON PARADE). (RUNS THIRTY FEET AWAY TO HUG FOUR KIDS WHO WAVED AT HIM). (FALLS TO THE GROUND AND SHAKES HIS ARMS AND LEGS IN UTTER JOY AND APPRECIATION.)"

- BUCKINGHAM U. BADGER, BELOVED
UNIVERSITY OF WISCONSIN-MADISON MASCOT

RINGO

Artist: Kari Fisher
Sponsor: Greater Madison Convention & Visitors Bureau Board of Directors

"Ringo" is the nickname of Rob Andringa, a close friend of the artist, who was diagnosed with stage 4 colon cancer in 2017. A former UW-Madison hockey player and co-captain, Rob lives and breathes all things Badger. This statue is dedicated to Ringo, his family and the challenges that they are facing.

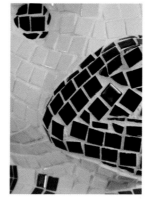

Artist: Tom Queoff
Sponsor: Clan Buchanan

Bucky is ready to lead the team to victory in his classic rugby gear. Rugby was first played on the UW-Madison campus in 1880 — hence the words "Rugby Since 1880" inscribed on the front.

SCONNIE B. GOODE

Artist: Michael Roberts
Sponsor: Badger Bus est. 1920

Sconnie B. Goode is an unusual mix of three areas — the artist's interest in vintage advertising and lettering (paper, fabric and tin), steampunk sculpture (metal and wood) and rustic Adirondack furniture (birch bark and twigs). As the artist gathered his materials, he noticed a strong theme of town names emerging — cities and towns from all over Wisconsin. The artist prefers to use vintage materials and originals in his work, especially when a large quantity of them are used together, like they were on Bucky.

Artist: Savannah Guthrie
Sponsor: Madison Area Sports Commission

From a distance, Bucky looks to be in his signature red and white striped sweater, but upon closer inspection, you'll see that over 4,000 community signatures are papier-mâchéd to the statue. This artist was inspired to create this piece to remind us of all the people in the Madison community and beyond who are united by their love for Bucky.

SPARK A DREAM

Artist: Barbara Westfall
Sponsor: American Family Insurance

This statue is adorned with numerous 'dream clouds' depicting American Family Insurance's mission of inspiring, protecting and restoring dreams. The clouds are connected by roads and paths surrounding the city of Madison, neighboring towns, parks and farms that make up the diversity of the area.

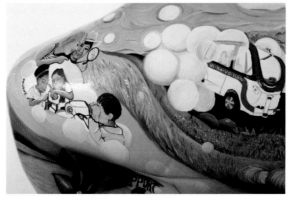

Pull up a chair and watch the light show over Madison's picturesque skyline. The artwork was created with acrylic paints and accented with glittery, glow-in-the-dark fireworks on the front and back.

SUNBURST

Artist: Jenny Steinman Heyden

DID YOU KNOW?

The colors of the iconic Sunburst chairs — John Deere green and Allis Chalmers orange and yellow — evoke spring, summer and fall while paying homage to Wisconsin farming traditions.

Sunburst combines a few of Madison's favorite sights: lakes and the famous Sunburst chair — two things you'll find at UW-Madison's Memorial Union Terrace. Come along, have a seat and savor the sweet summer feeling Sunburst brings to life.

Artists: Allyson Casey & Megan Breene
Sponsor: DeWitt Ross & Stevens S.C.

SUNSET

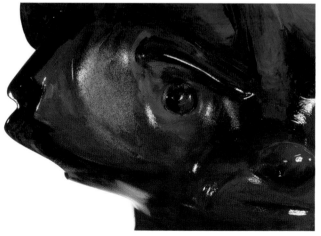

All the colors of a Memorial Union Terrace sunset come together in this beautiful statue, complete with the iconic Sunburst chair. Sunset was actually painted inside of the Union and spent the Parade there overlooking Lake Mendota.

SUPERBUCK

Artist: Rob Severson
Sponsor: Dr. Eric teDuits, Children's Dental Center of Madison, S.C.

This statue transforms Bucky into a superhero of epic proportions! The artist used a comic book style to create Bucky's alter ego, Superbuck.

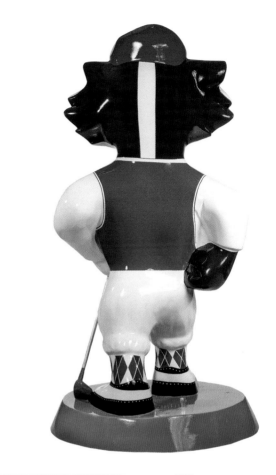

Bucky is ready to dominate on the golf course with his spiffy hat, argyle socks and Wisconsin vest. FAST Corporation is the premier manufacturer of fiberglass statues, roadside attractions, themed water slides and larger-than-life creations of all kinds. Along with manufacturing all the Bucky on Parade statues, FAST also painted several of them.

"BUCKY ON PARADE HAS DEFINITELY *put a spotlight* ON GARDING AGAINST CANCER AND RAISED AWARENESS FOR CANCER RESEARCH AND PATIENT CARE."

- GREG GARD, UW MEN'S BASKETBALL COACH AND GARDING AGAINST CANCER CO-FOUNDER

This upcycled Bucky is made from vial caps and other small plastics normally discarded during the course of patient care and surgery. Because the vial caps are so colorful, the artist began creating art with them as a rainy day project for her daughters. The logo on Bucky's chest represents his sponsor whose mission is printed around the base — For Research and Care. For a Cure. For Wisconsin. Garding Against Cancer raises money for cancer research and patient care around our great state. The cancer ribbons represent all cancers (lavender), cancer survivors (purple) and brain cancer (gray), which is placed in honor of Greg Gard's father. Gard is the head coach of the University of Wisconsin men's basketball team and his father's cancer journey was the inspiration for establishing Garding Against Cancer.

VINTAGE GRIDIRON

Artist: Paul Muckler
Sponsor: Zimbrick Honda

This Bucky statue salutes the proud heritage of University of Wisconsin football with a 1920s-style vintage uniform.

Greetings from Madison! This statue showcases all the wonderful things about Madison, from the bustling downtown to the beautiful lakes.

VISIBLE BUCKY

Artists: Philip Salamone with Sarah Gerg
Sponsor: Best Western PLUS InnTowner Madison

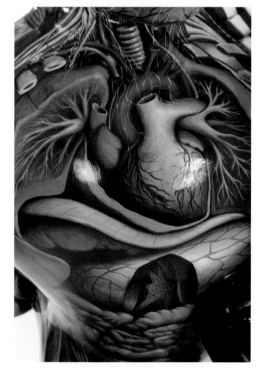

This design goes underneath the skin to show a fascinating glimpse at the skeleton and musculature beneath. It was fittingly located in front of UW-Madison's Science Hall during the Parade.

WE ALL FIT TOGETHER

Artist: Sara Nagreen
Sponsor: Sun Prairie Tourism Commission

White space brings order to the colorful chaos of this design. Organic figures slide together like puzzle pieces to seamlessly blanket Bucky. This statue allowed the artist to take a break from her IT career and explore her artistic side instead.

Artist: Kim Marie
Sponsor: Wipfli LLP

Program covers, ticket stubs, newspaper headlines and photos of fans were printed on archival paper and decoupaged over this entire Bucky statue.

WHEN YOU SAY WISCONSIN, YOU'VE SAID IT ALL

Artists: Hiebing Staff
Sponsor: Hiebing

Painted Badger red and covered with symbols of Wisconsin, including the Capitol, cows, forests and bicycles, this statue indeed says it all. The artwork was done by employees of Hiebing, who also sponsored the statue. They're diehard Badger fans and proud to call Madison home!

This statue brings the beauty of Wisconsin's Driftless Area to life, complete with a few cows. The marking on Bucky's forehead is done in the shape of Wisconsin. The artist grew up in Madison and as a child was told by her older brother that Bucky was the statue on top of the Capitol building!

WORK SAFE BUCKY

Artist: Danica Harrier
Sponsor: Tri-North Builders, Inc.

Bucky has his hard hat on and is ready for any job. This statue is inspired by the artist's occupation — helping employers make their work sites safer and healthier.

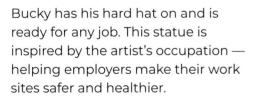

PARADE STATUE LOCATIONS

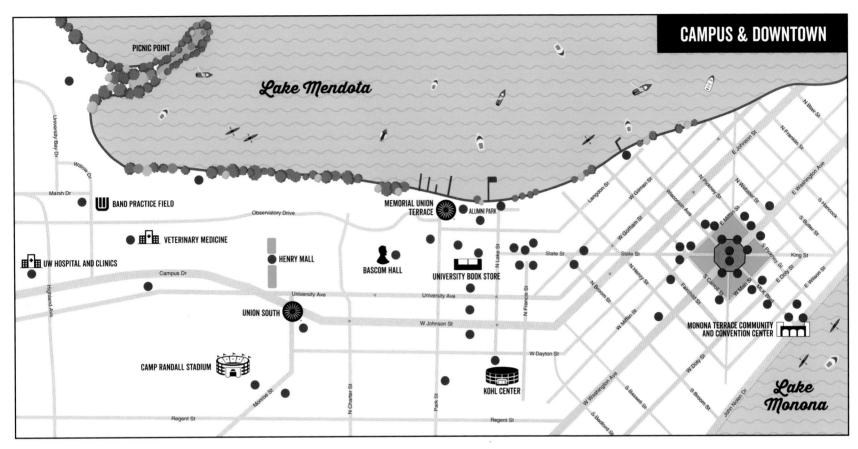

From Campus to Capitol, Middleton to Sun Prairie, and everywhere in between, Bucky on Parade statues were located all around Madison and Dane County. The widespread distribution allowed fans to not only enjoy the hunt to find all 85 statues, but also encouraged exploration of the city and beyond. The red dots on the map mark where the statues lived while on parade from May 7–September 12, 2018.

Visit buckyonparade.com for post-parade statue locations.

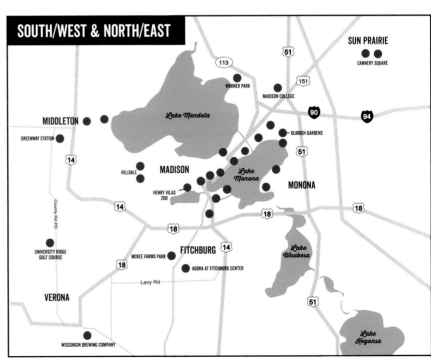

Special Thanks

With a project of this magnitude, it truly took a village to bring it to life. In addition to the Bucky on Parade project team, we'd like to give a special thanks to a few of the many others who were instrumental in making Bucky on Parade happen.

Chancellor Rebecca Blank, Vice Chancellor Charles Hoslet and Assistant Vice Chancellor Tricia Nolan from the University of Wisconsin for their support in this exciting community event.

The partners who worked tirelessly behind the scenes as we prepared to bring these statues to the streets of Madison and Dane County, including FAST Corporation, Madison College, Lycon, TWO MEN AND A TRUCK and JP Cullen. Your commitment inspired us.

Our parade partners, sponsors, artists and host locations for all 85 statues—Bucky on Parade wouldn't have been possible without you.

The Madison Area Sports Commission Board of Directors, under the leadership of our chair, Chris Armstrong.

The Greater Madison Convention & Visitors Bureau Board of Directors and Staff.

Focal Flame Photography for your dedication in documenting the year-long process.

Thank you to all of you and the countless others who supported this project, all for the love of Bucky.

BUCKY ON PARADE PROJECT TEAM

Project Lead
Kate Dale

Project Assistants
Ellen Larson
Amber Wiza

Executive Committee
Deb Archer, Chair
Joe Boucher, Chair
Turina Bakken
Lauren Birkel
Paula Bonner
Jane Clark
Justin Doherty
Nancy Francisco-Welke
Heather Garrison
Jim Kennedy
Tricia Nolan
Jeanette Riechers

Artist Recruitment Committee
Jeanette Riechers, Chair
Diane Morgenthaler, Staff Lead
Mark Fraire
Josette Jaucian
Danielle Lawry
Heather Owens
Jamie Patrick
Karin Wolf

Sponsorship Committee
Jane Clark, Chair
Kristin Wensing, Staff Lead
Kyle Buchmann
Heather Garrison
Marc Sherry
Scott Silvestri
Mike Unitan

Operations Committee
Lauren Birkel, Chair
Jamie Patrick, Staff Lead
Janine Wachter, Staff Lead
Megan Blake-Horst
Katie Crawley
Daniel Einstein
Greg Frank
Terry Gawlik
Nancy Hoffman
Brandon Holstein
Mark Ihlenfeldt
Jason Ilstrup
Tim Jenquin
Kelli Lamberty
Lisa Laschinger
Julie Murphy Agnew
Claire Oleksiak
Ted Peterson
Chris Petykowski
Laura Portz
Jason Rittel
Elise Ruoho
Darrin Smith

Marketing Committee
Turina Bakken, Chair
Kate Dale, Staff Lead
Ellen Larson, Staff Lead
Corinne Burgermeister
Rob Crain
Rob Gard
Tiffany Kenney
Kevin Kluender
Amy LaPlante
Angie Maniaci
Kevin Phelps
Corinn Ploessl
Ellen Roeder
Stacey Scannell
Jill Schmitz
Diane Stojanovich
Kristin Uttech

Greater Madison Convention & Visitors Bureau and Madison Area Sports Commission Staff:
Michelle Andler
Deb Archer
Julie Beauchamp
Monique Branch
Rick Bristol
Sarah Buob
Corinne Burgermeister
Ann Custer
Kate Dale
Michael Fiez
Jon Freund
Rob Gard
Carolyn Greene
Kate Hartmann
Lisa Hasenbalg
Debbie Hines
Jeff Holcomb
Brandon Holstein
Amy LaPlante
Ellen Larson
John Leinen
Sarah Lemmers
Katrin Madayag-Ard
Tyler Marlow
Maureen Martin
Diane Morgenthaler
Jamie Patrick
Corinn Ploessl
Laura Portz
Eric Reichert
Jordan Rodewald
Kathleen Ripp
Anna Shircel
Nicole Slemin
Colleen Sovey
Bekah Stauffacher
Julie Vanden Brook
Janine Wachter
Emily Wendt
Kristin Wensing
Amber Wiza

PARADE SNAPSHOTS

All 85 Bucky on Parade statues marched their way into the hearts of fans of every age and greater Madison embraced (literally!) them with an undeniably contagious passion. From marriage proposals, to graduations and family reunions, the Buckys temporarily became part of the community and shared countless special moments during the summer of 2018. Thank you so much to the fans — locals and visitors alike — who spent hours looking for Buckys. It was remarkable to see everyone who dedicated themselves to finding all 85 statues and shared their love for Bucky with family members and friends. The Parade would not have been a success without you!

Becky Blank @BeckyBlank · Aug 17
Bucky is more than a mascot— he's a symbol of our great university. I'm proud to see him all around Madison as part of @BuckyOnParade chancellor.wisc.edu/blog/more-than... #buckyonparade

Marsha Meisel Mood My son and I had a great time hunting for Buckys! We are both graduates of UW-Madison (me in 1973, him in 2005) and it was especially fun to find the Buckys on campus! Thanks so much for this amazing public art event. P.S. We found all 85 of them! 🤍

Wisconsin Colors

JUMP AROUND

Jeana Schneider We came from Green Bay for a day to share our favorite city with our daughters 9 & 6. They LOVED seeing all the Buckys! We had so much fun searching for our favorites and spotting others on the way. Showing the girls more of the city than they have seen was awesome for us. Pretty sure we have sealed the deal...they both want to go to UW Madison!!!! 🖤

Like · Reply · Message · 1d · Edited   👍 2

Fitchburg Bio-Tech Buck

Lisa Harms ▶ Bucky on Parade
July 8 · 🌐

We did it! We found all 84 (waiting patiently for Crazylegs Bucky) Buckys! What a fun, family activity that got us out and about the area. We celebrated our accomplishment with a commemorative mini Golden Bucky statue! Thanks for a wonderful hunt!

Kristie Konsoer @kkbadger1 · Aug 16
Worth the climb up Bascom Hill to see Graduation Bucky.
So proud to be a UW-Madison alum.
@BuckyOnParade @UWMadison

Candice Poff Larson ▶ Bucky on Parade
Yesterday

We've had fun exploring Madison looking for Bucky & finding other fun things along the way.

Tiffany Geist added 8 new photos to the album: Summer Bucky List — with Jesse Geist.
August 13 at 6:04 PM · 🌐

8 more Bucky's checked off the list today!!!
We have plans this week to see the remaining 5, and then we will have seen them ALL!

Shout out to Bucky on Parade for helping us make amazing summer memories, and letting us get to know this beautiful city a little more!...
See More

Jill Boggs Doering ▶ Bucky on Parade
July 16 ·

My daughter and I have started finding Buckys. We are up to 42. This is so
much fun and a great way for us to spend time together!

Jonathan Cue @cuemancue · 20h
Art, authentic school spirit and a treasure map - what more could you want?
#buckyonparade
#loveart @ Madison, Wisconsin instagram.com/p/Bmrfexbhv-7U...

INDEX BY *Statue*

THE ORGANIZATIONS BEHIND BUCKY ON PARADE

The Madison Area Sports Commission was the producer of Bucky on Parade, with support from the Greater Madison Convention & Visitors Bureau and in partnership with the University of Wisconsin–Madison, University of Wisconsin Athletics and Wisconsin Foundation & Alumni Association. Event proceeds support non-profit organizations such as Garding Against Cancer, the Madison Area Sports Commission and other community charities.

The Madison Area Sports Commission

The Madison Area Sports Commission (MASC) is the greater Madison area's official sports marketing organization. Launched by the Greater Madison Convention & Visitors Bureau in 2010, MASC is charged with elevating the recognition and awareness of greater Madison as a sports event destination and the positive impact of sports tourism on the regional economy, while serving the unique needs of the sports tourism industry. From international events like the CrossFit Games to longtime favorites like IRONMAN WI, niche sports like tug of war to imaginative offerings like quidditch, MASC serves as Madison's host to the global sporting community. MASC also works to help local organizations expand their impact on underserved communities through its youth sports grants. For more information about MASC, visit madisonsports.org.

The Greater Madison Convention & Visitors Bureau

The Greater Madison Convention & Visitors Bureau (GMCVB) plays a key role in supporting the more than 21,000 Dane County residents who work in the tourism and hospitality industry. Promoting tourism in Madison since 1972, the GMCVB provides the framework for the more than $2 billion dollars generated by visitor spending in Dane County every year. The GMCVB creates opportunities for local businesses and organizations to connect with visitors, and helps people from all over the world feel like they are part of the Madison community during their visit. For the most up-to-date information, go to visitmadison.com.

The University of Wisconsin-Madison

The University of Wisconsin–Madison is a public, land-grant institution that offers a complete spectrum of studies through 13 schools and colleges. With more than 43,000 students from every U.S. state and 121 countries, UW–Madison is the flagship campus of Wisconsin's state university system. UW–Madison is a formidable research engine, ranking sixth among U.S. universities as measured by dollars spent on research. Faculty, staff and students are motivated by a tradition known as the Wisconsin Idea that the boundaries of the university are the boundaries of the state and beyond.

Garding Against Cancer

Partnering with the University of Wisconsin and the Wisconsin Foundation and Alumni Association, Garding Against Cancer's mission is to philanthropically support the cancer-fighting community throughout the state of Wisconsin. Garding Against Cancer generously provides funds to those in the medical field who have made it their lives' work to find a cure and/or better treatment options for patients battling cancer. Garding Against Cancer compassionately promotes the welfare of people with a cancer diagnosis as well as the benevolent families and friends who support them. All funds raised by Garding Against Cancer stay in Wisconsin, making the most positive impact on current and future residents of the state. For more information please visit gardingagainstcancer.org.

YOU'VE NEVER SEEN BUCKY LIKE *This* BEFORE.